YOUR FIRST STARTUP

The Startup Business Guide, From Idea To Launch

WAYNE ST. A. WALKER

Table of Contents

Disclaimer

The advice and strategies contained in this guide are based on my personal business experiences and opinions, and may not be appropriate for your situation.

Introduction

My motivation for writing this guide is similar to my other works, where I know from practical experience that you do <u>not</u> need 200 pages to explain to someone how to do something successfully. Being the owner of a profitable business I also know, from experience, that I do not need 200 pages to share the essence of running a business. Many might disagree but I am not concerned with them at the moment. I am a big believer in Gandhi's quote, "an ounce of practice is worth more than tons of preaching."

Wayne Walker (the short version)

For my words and ideas to have more meaning a quick overview of my background is essential. I am the Director and Owner of GCMS, a capital markets consulting and training firm.

This is not an autobiography (I am way too young). The quick version, born in Jamaica, W.I. and raised in New York City to parents who did the best they could with the tools they had. Like many others of their generation they sacrificed so that their children could have opportunities that were unavailable to them and I am forever grateful. I attended university in Buffalo, New York and San Diego, California.

I currently reside in Europe, which is an adventure of its own, material for my third guide. I thought socialism was erased from the planet but to my amazement it is alive and well, giving *some* people a free ride because they are entitled to everything for "free".

Prior to starting the firm I was the head of teams of Investment Advisors at Saxo Bank (Copenhagen) one of the pioneers in online investment banking and electronic trading. It was truly a special place to work. Every day was literally better than the day before. People made good and in some cases very generous salaries.

I was the 140th employee in a bank that grew to about 1,500 at my resignation. Needless to say, I saw a lot of new faces. The people I met were absolutely amazing. I still collaborate with many ex-Saxo guys on projects.

We worked hard and played hard. Yes, very long hours were put in but I/my family also gladly enjoyed the fruits of it, so it is a little late to complain. Family challenges are a part of the investment banking lifestyle, which I was swimming in every chance I could get. I held seminars in the beautiful Caribbean, trained Citi - FX staff in London, even did seminars in Hollywood. The nightlife remains a closed book.

My time at Saxo Bank was one of immense learning and in the end I resigned on good terms and who knows I might collaborate with them in the future.

Starting a business has been a dream of mine and with some savings I ventured out on my own.

WHERE TO BEGIN

Scalable

The idea of whatever you have in mind must, must be scalable. Meaning that you your business can handle an order for 1,000 units with almost the same ease as a 100. I am taking some liberty here with the numbers, but the point is that it should be able to expand without needing a 1:1 ratio. So that if with 10 orders you need 10 employees and so on.

The Saxo Bank secret? They mastered the art of scaling.

Is your idea scalable? You can't run from this, unless you can scale your idea you simply have created a job and not a business. If this isn't figured out, keep your day job until you have a plan.

Using GCMS as an example it began as a one man operation in EU, along with staff in the Caribbean leading the operations and back office. We started out with holding seminars which is a form of scaling. A seminar allows me to service many clients at once. Teaching them one on one is not feasible unless of course you have the situation where each client is paying thousands of dollars and you have a stream of them.

Review your idea, how can you spread it so that it's not necessary for you to be involved with it 24/7. One of the easiest ways to scale is by having an employee, or having paid or performance based pay consultants. They can spread your idea faster than you can alone. These persons also have networks that can be exploited for everyone's benefit. In GCMS's case one consultant on our team had many media and university contacts. At the startup phase this access to free media was a huge blessing for us (more on this later).

Think about all the wave of internet entrepreneurs who have made fortunes over the years, they have scaled their concept. A website works 24/7 taking orders while you sleep, ski, or party, I think you are getting the point.

Whether you are a great banker, webmaster, massage therapist or cook, unless you can spread your ideas out without much personal involvement, keep your job and save yourself and family the stress.

Specialized hand-made jewelry for example will be very difficult to scale. To be fair it is not an impossible idea, because if your name is famous enough and you can sell each piece for a million Euros profit, then scaling is not an issue. Unfortunately, the majority of us do not have the type of name recognition needed to move expensive jewelry with ease.

This might sound basic but this is critical or else it is really difficult to move on. I share my personal experience with my own business that many parts are scalable but it is not 100%. That is a challenge that I am also working with.

There are many practical example of this in the real world, for example many fast food places. If a local franchise jumps from serving 100 burgers to 200 burgers an hour they don't hire an extra 100 employees.

The good news is there are many ideas that can be scaled especially with the internet. They also do not need huge amounts of capital. Many people have explored the reselling concept and it has worked out great for them where they have a site selling products 24 hours a day with an automatic billing system. Therefore 100 orders or a 1,000 requires the same effort.

In my firm GCMS we live these principles by scaling our e-guides. On the website we are open 24/7 for orders and they get processed without me sitting at my computer day & night. We have an order form that takes the information needed, and an automatic email that is returned.

Our classes we can teach 25-40 people with the same amount of instructors, while maintaining the quality level needed.

Focus

It has been said many times, you can't be all things to all people and in business it is very true. Attempting to specialize in Italian and Chinese food in the same restaurant is a recipe for failure (I actually saw this restaurant during my travels through America)

You must find an area where you can bring value to people. Either in a product or service (that is of course scalable)

I have a friend who owns a business where he "specializes" in just about every type of art genre (audio, furniture, paintings, etc.). I have suggested repeatedly that he finds an area to excel in first, and then introduce to clients the other things he is good at. 10

years into his business and it has not risen above a hobby status, in regards to revenue.

It is difficult to find examples of any firm finding success by initially attempting to capture many markets. Most will find one region, product, or service to be good at first and then release other services as time goes on.

In my experience with GCMS, it was only after we began to focus that we started to see improved results. At first we were all over the place attempting to cater to all markets. Learn from my wasted efforts, money, and time, you must focus, focus, focus.

It was the success of our Trading Diploma program that gave us the push to be seen by others outsides of the university market. We teach at top universities but a sizable portion of our attendees are not students. They helped us expand by word of mouth to the professional community.

This e-guide is another example of focus, I believe that there is a market of people who want to learn things by getting straight to the point. I am not a university professor, but I have practical experience that can be shared without someone needing a lifetime of study. Therefore I create guides that are hands-on and can be read in minutes or a few hours. The benefit is that they can be used immediately as practical reference materials for those that purchase the guides. Once the diploma program was a success then we were able to release the e-guide, CV services, etc.

Get Talked About

Having people talking about you or your business is key to profits in the long run. Even if it means making less money in the beginning. The GCMS example is classic basic word-of-mouth marketing. We own our content but we unfortunately did not have millions to use on advertising.

We focused first on delivering a good product that people would want to share/recommend to their friends. The first step we did was to partner with groups who had access to distribution. Our initial partner was University College of the Caribbean. They gave us access to finance professionals in the region without us having to spend money on marketing.

Our next partner was Finance Lab in Copenhagen which was able to connect us with university students, initially in Copenhagen and later to the rest of Denmark. These connections gave us instant distribution and got people talking about us. There is no overnight magic, it does take time in the beginning but once you get a little momentum, then things really can start rolling quickly. This is a basic technique that we are replicating with many groups that has lead to more organic growth for our firm, but it does take time. Of course our service must deliver a value to clients, or else no group, connections, or marketing can save you long term.

Getting in the press, someone to write about you is best for instant attention. After a few articles about GCMS appeared in several newspapers the visits to our website jumped by over 400%.

The one thing that was a complete waste of time and money in the beginning, was attempting to advertise in newspapers, online ads, etc. Listen to me and the many others who has made this foolish mistake…save your money for other things. The so-called gurus internet marketing "pros" <u>forget them</u>, unless they can show you the business that they are running by using the techniques that they suggest for you. More on these guys later in the guide.

Seth Godin, author of *Purple Cow*, stresses that the bottom line in getting talked about, is assisting people in achieving their goals, so that over time they will have a vested interest in helping you to reach yours. I can confirm from practical experience that this is true.

Holding myself true to my word, only things that I have done that actually worked for GCMS or I have seen working for others will be discussed. At the end of the guide, my contact details are provided & I can discuss/verify any suggestion that I have made.

Good People

In the beginning surrounding yourself with capable and positive people is critical. Starting a business, let's say it straight out, is tough, tough even if you have the "perfect" idea. Having people who will tell what needs to be said without being afraid is a gift more valuable than money. The free but invaluable advice that my good friends and our advisory board shared with me was great.

Without mercy, eliminate all negative people. Do not confuse this with constructive criticism. My rule with people is, if you critique, you must have an alternative suggestion. Saying "your website sucks" is useless, unless you have concrete suggestion on how to improve it. Better yet, impress me with your website that includes all the features that you suggested are lacking in mine.

I had people close to me who probably would benefit the most from the results of starting my firm and instead of being in the support column they wasted their time and mine by being negative. A warning to budding entrepreneurs, you are on your own. To be fair, it is not your friends or family's job to save your business. If they assist, great, but they are under no obligations, in my opinion, to help you, but they should stay clearly out of your way and not be a nuisance.

The Mental

Never, never, give up. As a few smart people have correctly said, either give up in the beginning or you have to ride the journey out to the end. Whenever you set out to make a change in your life, like starting a business, you should expect turbulence, it is part of the process.

Simply put, you will have paid the sacrifice in time, money, effort without getting any of the gains if you quit half way. There will be dark days, in my case, many, but the belief in myself and my idea kept me going. By not giving up, you will notice that over time, the opposition (negative people and thoughts) will fade away. And the self –defeating tendencies that many of us have will become weaker.

This mental discipline must be trained and developed. Your mental state is the most crucial component in the beginning. Many people when talking about starting a business will focus on the business plan and overlook their mental plan. Don't make that mistake.

In your climb to the goal, remember that just because things did not happen exactly according to the time schedule, it is not a sign of failure. For many, success came after the point when everyone thought things were hopeless. Not quite so dramatic in my case but things did begin to change after the personal deadline I had set for the business to be running with a profit.

You must ask yourself two questions and have very good answers to them before pulling the trigger to begin:

1-Are you afraid to make mistakes?

You will make plenty, if this is a problem area for you, seek emotional counseling before beginning.

2- How far are you willing to go to see your idea through to the end?

Starting a business will test you in every way imaginable, so be prepared.

Concrete things that I did to keep functioning mentally:

Exercising

It is the world's best high. After a heavy session in the gym, I have the physical and mental energy to fight on. You pick the sport, but move your body. Many recent studies state that one of the few things proven to increase brain power is exercise. I am a believer.

Writing

Writing gave me an opportunity to get mind off business for a few hours at a time. It is also a great way to learn how to assemble your thoughts in some sort of structure.

Reading

I flew often between North America and Europe in the first year of the firm which provide a lot of "dead" hours. Reading stories of how others overcame adversity was of great mental help. While all of our stories are unique, challenges similar to ours have been faced by others and it is good to learn from them. It will save you much trial and error time. As stated before, read from those who have done it, save theory for the lecture hall.

WHAT CONSULTANTS WON'T TELL YOU

Income

I recently read an article that mentioned having too much money when starting a firm is a danger. There are valid points in that idea, but it would have been easier sleeping if I had more at the start.

Be ready for income swings that would scare any gambler. In the beginning there might be none at all. In my case there was no positive income until after the first year. Meaning that there were revenues, but expenses exceeded them. Then when it does start to flow it can take nice jumps and then steady into an average.

How did I deal with it? Used a bit of my savings and turning to acting and modeling. I was lucky enough that I have modeled on and off for many years. The Danish Royal Theater called me for a supporting role in a play and I jumped at the chance. Not mega dollars but it covered many of my expenses.

Any prospective business owner, especially those with limited means should have in the back of their minds a way for generating survival money until your firm takes off. No shame in flipping burgers if it keeps the roof over your head. There are so many stories of people sleeping on their friends' sofas for months at a time during the lean times, be prepared for it.

We live in wonderful times where it doesn't take a huge amount of capital to start a business thanks to the internet. However, since the barrier of entry has been lowered, it also means the competition has intensified.

Expenses

Keep a close eye on them as they can be a silent killer. If you have staff, then another layer of vigilance is needed. Not that they have evil intentions, but more likely that they do not have the same investment in the firm as you. This in some cases leads to them being far more relaxed with vendors than you are comfortable with. For example, they will order more than what is needed or something that is simply not needed.

Friends - Private Life

Be prepared to be alone. Be prepared to be alone. Not a typo, I wanted to make sure that the point gets through. If you have problem with spending time alone, keep your day job and go home to your family.

Your "friends" for the most part, will disappear faster than you will ever believe. Be prepared for the people who say "you can count on me", "call me if you need anything", just vanishing. Forget it, 98% clearly do not mean it.

Your real friends, the few that remain (the 2%), while amazing can't do it for you and it is also not their responsibility.

As for family, don't expect too much support there either. In my case my brother was a first supporter on my idea and I am grateful to him for backing me from the start.

For those who are married, obviously you must have 100% backing from your spouse or get ready for turbulence at home.

You will spend many hours and in some cases days alone when you feel it is all a waste, but getting bitter or sad is a waste of time. Use the tools mentioned above to deal with it. Exercise is my favorite and it does wonders for your self-esteem.

Your private life will take a hit. Basically I had none, I don't think I had one date for over a year. Actually I was quite happy about it, as it gave me a chance to focus. I must also admit it would have been great to have partner in the process to share some of the moments with. I am sure some of my friends probably started to worry about me, but I was doing fine. Those of you with girlfriends/boyfriends, be very careful. If there is ever a time that you are at a risk for splitting up this is it.

Consultants

Run from these clowns as if your life depended on it, <u>unless</u>, they have done what they are consulting about. I do not want to over generalize, but the majority of consultants are absolutely useless. They come with lots of charts, power point slides, and all the idiotic buzz words of the moment, but when it comes to results (the only thing that matters) they are often lacking.

I was fortunate to come across a few of the good guys in the business and I gladly share their services with others, as I know these people can deliver results.

Internet marketing "experts"

Consultants are risky, but these internet guys are the worst. Forget them period. Work only with those that have run a business that made/makes a profit. Ignore all the nonsense about running ad campaigns if you are small business owner.

The way to market is, to be talked about. Word of mouth is the best by far. These "pros" will try to tell otherwise, but I can confirm from real business experience this is the way to build a business that will be around. If your goal is to create a new business every few months, then this might not be the strategy for you as it does take time to build a solid business. Review the techniques that I discussed earlier of using partners that can provide you with distribution access.

Consultants of all kinds must be able to show you examples of how this expertise or brilliance that they claim they possess has helped others or themselves. Preferably in the same or related sector as the business that you are looking to enter.

On another personal note, my father ran a successful tax advising business from our family home in New York City without scaling. How did he do it? He scaled his "advertising". My father, in over 20 years of business has never spent a dollar on advertising. His clients filled him with referrals (because of excellent service and a fair fee), often he was turning people away because of business overload. Amazingly it was done without the internet or any "marketing gurus".

Now there is no contradiction in my concepts, I said he was forced to turn away clients. This is because he did not scale, while he did well financially, there was only so far he could grow. The way forward for him of course, was to put some services on the web and hire staff to help with some of the routine issues.

OTHER PRACTICAL MATTERS

The Business Plan

Most books or advisors will tell you to write one, and banks will demand one. My view on it is like investing, it is very personal. It doesn't hurt in the sense that it helps with the planning, but I am big believer in just let us get started. You will spend the rest of your precious life waiting for the "perfect" moment. Trust me, you will encounter these non- accomplishment clowns with their advice of waiting for this magic moment. Examine their lives and usually they haven't accomplished much after leaving grade school. Many of us have amazing ideas, but because we are afraid to fail, we don't even try.

I would recommend a SWOT analysis even if you don't go with the 50 page business plan (which few actually read). For those who skipped business school, SWOT = (Strength, is it scalable?, Weakness, Opportunities, Threats). This is a great reality check for *you*, not the banks or your friends.

As I have heard, "think big, but start small", this is the way forward for many unless you have very deep pockets. Even if you do, I would suggest starting small any way.

Legal & Regulatory Issues

Get all the necessary permits but before getting yourself into any trouble. Later on if you seek funding then it's good to have these. Some say you should also get an attorney, and depending on the type of business you want to start it's a good idea. If it is a partnership or you are holding people's money for ex. to trade, then get an attorney. If you have a good scalable idea that you can handle I say run with it. The theme I repeat is getting started, and you will just have to deal with things as they come along, the magic moment doesn't exist.

An attorney might be optional but an accountant is not, you must have one. The one we have has saved us thousands and helped us to keep on track. I freely admit, like most business owner types, I am not crazy about this aspect of running a business but it must be handled. Luckily there are millions of people in the world who enjoy looking at tax codes and being compliant.

Dealing With Banks

This is another potential area of disappointment. From the horror stories I have heard from other business owners, I often wonder what purpose banks serve.

I must say, I started my business at probably the worst time in modern financial history, fall 2008. Even with excellent credit, money in the bank, and being a client for many years I was quickly denied a business loan. At other banks they didn't even want to hear from me. They wanted a sure thing, starting a business is far from it. I have tried my best not to take it personal because I shouldn't, but it was still a bitter taste.

My advice, if you need a loan is to try. Just because it was no for me it does not mean a no for you.

On Offering Your Service For Free

Forget it! Even if you only charge a dollar it's better than free. People find it hard to value free services and when you attempt to charge for what was free it gets messy. At one point I considered giving away my first e-guide and nothing came of it. I started to sell them and people starting buying.

Offering Credit

Not possible. Offering credit can turn your young business into a hostage to all types of private and corporate clients. At GCMS we had a few unpleasant experiences with a few private clients, since switching to payment upfront business increased and headaches decreased.

Partners

As with a spouse select them carefully. My experience with partners has been pretty good to date. One should be aware of the so called serial entrepreneurs. Since their commitment levels can be questionable, work with people who are willing to go the distance with and for you.

Be extra careful with those that you share your ideas with. Unfortunately I had the nasty experience of sharing a key component of GCMS with some potential business partners. They mentioned that my idea while good, would not sell. Sure enough a month later they launched a business based on my idea that they said would *never* work.

A legal Suggestion:

When you have a great idea, write it down and mail it to yourself. The date on the stamp may prove crucial in Intellectual Property related disputes, as YOU will be able to prove that you had the idea first....Just remember to keep the envelope sealed. Stick on a post-it note with what it contains if needed.

IT

My personal weak area, so I did consult with others. Basically I have all data backed up on multiple computers and also online. All you need is one data loss experience to learn the lesson needed. Use my experience, back things up frequently.

I also strongly suggest that you have two laptops when travelling far from home. I have had situations where computers refused to start or connections with projectors, etc., suddenly did not work. Having that extra laptop proved to be a lifesaver.

Website

Your website must have a CMS (Content Management System). This allows you to do most of the site updating yourself, eliminating a potential bottleneck area. The CMS also provides you with access to site traffic data (who visited, from where, language, what pages they looked at, etc.). This can assist you with your marketing strategy.

Social Media

A tricky topic. If you are planning to run a night club, DJ business, café, etc. then Facebook ,Twitter, etc. might be of help. But as I mentioned, be careful of these social media "gurus" telling you that you need to be everywhere. The one service that I have found to provide some value is Linkedin. There is more professionalism and you avoid much of the silliness of other social media and the spamming.

I suggest that business owners should focus on in-person social media by meeting at network events. Then you can lead people to your site. Word of mouth is still powerful even in the 21st century

Keep in mind the points I have touched on at the start; focus, and get talked about. You have only 24 hours to the day so you must focus on one medium to get the best return for your time and effort.

WHAT KIND OF BUSINESS TO START?

I strongly suggest you examine business ideas that do not need much physical space. The goal is to avoid having to rent space and all the expenses that come along with it, for example extra utility bills. Any type of restaurant, clothing store, etc. are not recommended for the low budget potential business owner.

Avoid the urge to follow the silly trends of the moment. Focus on scalable business ideas that deliver practical benefits to people at a reasonable price.

E-Books

If you have practical information to share with people, this is a good angle. People will pay for valuable information that they can put to use relatively quickly.

When your book is ready for sale, with some of the biggest players in the business. I have also gone the way of selling my books directly from my website. I am able to do this because have my own website and I wanted to keep the profits of my work for myself. However my book is still available for sale on several sites but the majority of my sales are generated from my own websites.

Webinars-Online Classes

Delivering paid webinars, classes, etc. people pay for access to your knowledge. I have coached people globally and it is lucrative and personally satisfying. You will feel a sense of satisfaction knowing that you have helped someone to solve a problem or opened new possibilities for them.

Consulting

People will pay for your knowledge if you can demonstrate how your knowledge and skill will benefit them in a practical way. I work with people on delivering practical education about the capital markets & straight talk about the reality of starting a business with limited cash

NEXT STEP

When You Are Ready To Begin – Contact me

I sincerely hope that this practical & brief guide was of benefit to you. However, I also realize that an e-guide does have some limitations. For those that would like more hands-on coaching please contact me at: gcmsonline.info . There is also a help desk type function where I or my colleagues respond directly to your business challenges.

SWOT Analysis

This SWOT analysis can be used as reference. I used this in year one of my firm. A few details remain secret but a lot of what I examined at the start of GCMS is open for review.

Location of Headquarters

Headquarters of the firm is located in Copenhagen.

SWOT Analysis

Strengths

- **Management:** Our management staff is internationally experienced and highly skilled in their specific field.

- **Knowledgeable staff:** Our pool of consultants includes some of the best in the business.

- **Clear vision of the market need:** GCMS knows its potential clients(private traders, large and medium sized financial institutions)

Weaknesses

- **Financing:** Preliminary overview of expenditures suggest that GCMS will remain financially stable. However, unforeseen expenditures or poor inflow of capital from sales might threaten GCMS cash position, which will be particularly vulnerable in the first year.

- **Limited Personnel:** Though GCMS staff is exceptional, they will be faced with long hours for little pay during the first year.

Opportunities

- **Growth in market:** The growing trend of the finance industry and developing markets in general will raise the number of potential clients for our services. After gaining stability, GCMS will focus on expanding our markets.

- **Potential to grow international:** As GCMS establishes itself and gains financial stability; it can begin to market its service in different developing countries. GCMS has started this campaign and we already have a physical presence on three continents. We will diversify our communications efforts additionally through the Internet.

- **Potential to become the foremost provider:** GCMS has not only the management and staff, it also has a scalable strategy from which to build a sustainable platform for growth.

Threats

- **Local competition:** There is no other provider of our service in Copenhagen or in our target market areas that specializes in what we do.

- **Emerging local competitors:** Currently, GCMS enjoys a first-mover advantage in the local markets. However, competitors might be on the horizon, and we are prepared for their entry. Many of our programs are built on expertise and <u>personal contacts that are simply not available to others</u>.

- **Laws, regulations, policies:** Any new legal requirements that GCMS might be required to adapt to.

- **Economic Downturn:** Unforeseen or unanticipated economic recession or tragedies like September 11th, would reduce disposable income.

Vision

GCMS has the potential and plans to become the foremost provider of capital markets education and consulting globally.

Profile of the Author

Wayne Walker is the Director of a global capital markets education and consulting firm(gcmsonline.info). He has several years experience in leading and coaching teams of Investment Advisors and has managed top performing teams in the Private Client Group based on Bench Mark Earnings (BME). Mr. Walker has trained traders of the Citi-FX Pro program in London. He also developed the 'Trading Rights' program at Saxo Bank by which Investment Advisors were required to complete before being allowed to trade. He is a certified trader by Markets in Financial Instrument Directive (MiFID) EU and is qualified to advise "A" clients.

Mr. Walker is a frequently invited guest capital markets commentator on several live international TV & radio programs.

Mr. Walker holds several certifications and has worked in the following positions:

- Director-Founder, (GCMS) Global Capital Market Solutions, Denmark

- Author of *Reality Based Trading Guide,(used in our classes at Copenhagen Business School & other universities in EU)*

- Manager, Sales Trading, North America & Middle East, Saxo Bank, Denmark

- B.sc State University of New York, College at Buffalo, USA

- NASD Series 3 - License to trade & advise on futures contracts in the US Market

- ACI(Financial Markets) Dealing Certificate - Passed with Distinction (highest level), France

- Trained in Bloomberg & UBS Bank's FX Options quoting software